Hustling and Bustling
CARS

WHEELS AND AUTOMOBILES

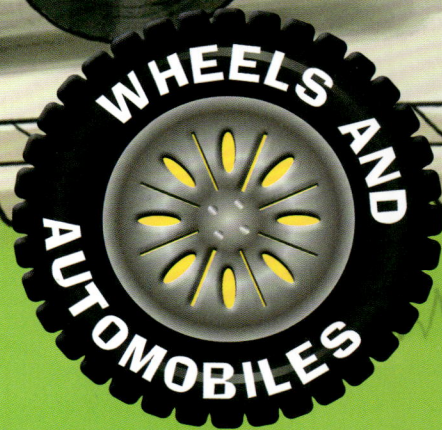

FOX EYE
PUBLISHING

A car is a machine that helps us to get around.

Some cars are super-speedy.
They whizz across the ground!

Some cars are wide. Some cars are long.
Some are really rather small.

How many cars can you see in this picture?
Can you count them all?

engine

All cars have an engine.
It gives them the power to go.

When some cars go quickly,
they can make quite a show!

wheel

A car has four wheels.
Two are found at the front.

Two more are at the rear.
All four help the car get into gear!

A car also has a steering wheel.
It makes the car turn left or right.

steering wheel

Around the bends and up the streets,
it makes driving a treat!

headlight

When the brake lights glow, other drivers know that the car ahead will start to slow. At the front of the car are two headlights.

brake light

Headlights help drivers to see at night.
The indicators are on both sides.
They flash when the car turns left or right.

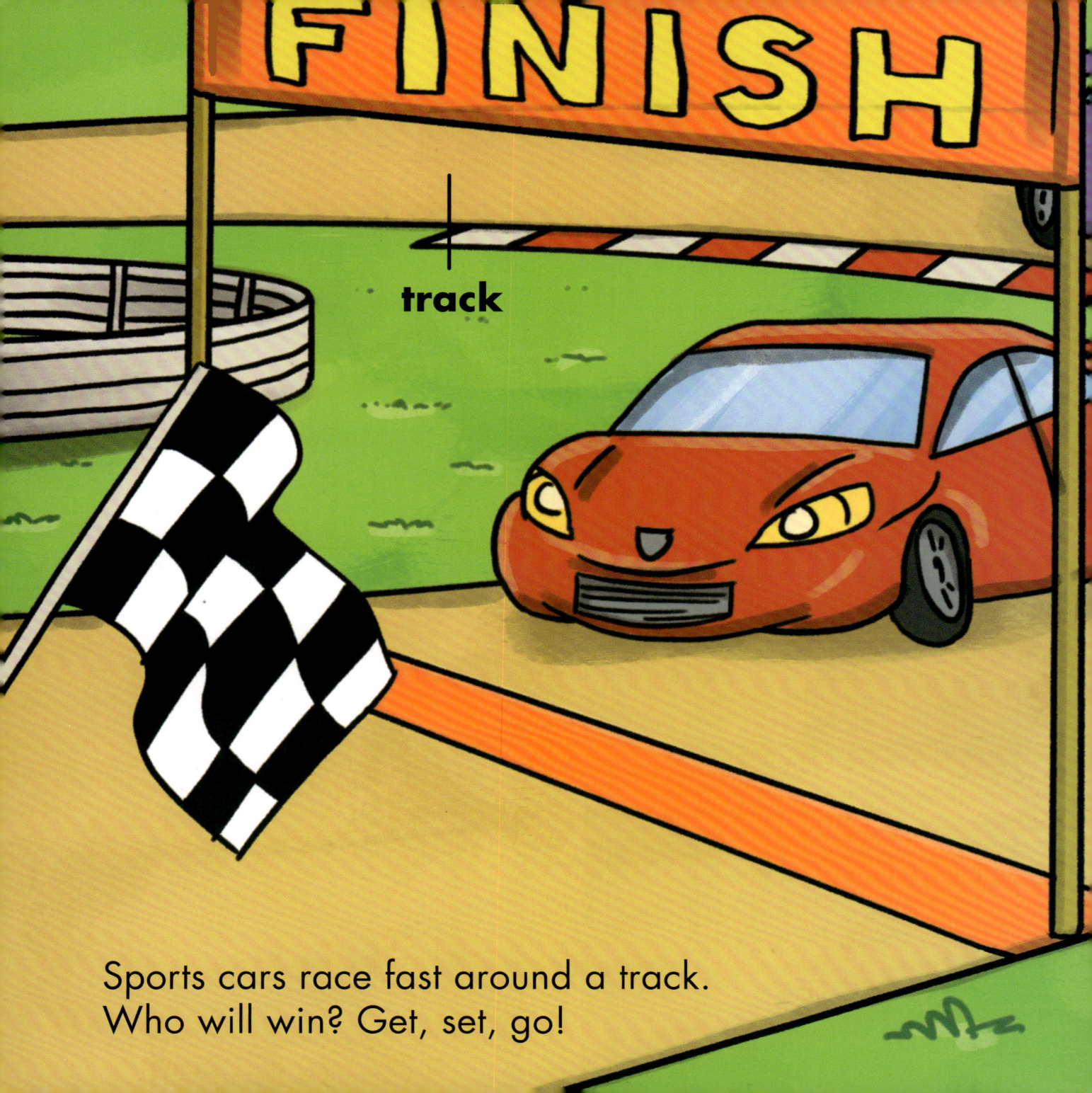

FINISH

track

Sports cars race fast around a track.
Who will win? Get, set, go!

sports car

The accelerator pedal makes them faster.
On the bends, the brake pedal help them slow.

roll cage

Off-road cars are strong and tough.
They drive over rough land with no roads.

Inside the car, there is a roll cage.
It protects the driver if the car rolls.

Large chunky wheels help off-road cars
to grip on mud, sand, ice and snow.

These cars are in an off-road rally.
They are racing fast. Look at them go!

Driving a car can be an adventure,
whether in sun, rain or snow.

At last, the adventurers return home for tea.
What will tomorrow's adventure be?

Bustling Words

An **accelerator pedal** makes a car go faster when it is pressed.

Brake lights are lights at the back of a car. They light up red when the car is slowing
or stopping.

A **brake pedal** makes a car go slower when it is pressed.

An **engine** is part of a car that makes its energy.

Get into gear means to get into a gear, or a speed that the car must travel at.

Headlights are lights at the front of a car. In the dark, they shine on the road like torches.

Indicator lights are small lights at the front and the back of a car. They flash to show that the car will turn.

A **machine** helps us to do work.

An **off-road rally** is a race over land that has no roads.

Power is energy to do something.

A **roll cage** is a frame of metal tubes inside the car. It makes the car stronger.

A **track** is a road in the shape of a circle. Sports cars race around it.

First published in 2024 by Fox Eye Publishing
Unit 31, Vulcan House Business Centre,
Vulcan Road, Leicester, LE5 3EF
www.foxeyepublishing.com

Author: Katherine Eason
Art director: Paul Phillips
Cover designer: Emma Bailey
Editor: Jenny Rush

All illustrations by Eszter Szepvolgyi

978-1-80445-338-4

Printed in China